·SUPERBOOK·

ANIMALS

RON TAYLOR

Kingfisher Books

Contents

Kingfisher Books, Grisewood & Dempsey Ltd,
Elsley House, 24-30 Great Titchfield Street,
London W1P 7AD

This revised edition published in 1985 by Kingfisher Books
Originally published in 1981 in hard cover by Ward Lock Limited
in the *Wonder Book* series.
10 9 8 7 6 5 4

British Library Cataloguing in Publication Data
A catalogue record for this book is available from
the British Library

ISBN 0-86272-179-2

Edited by Angela Royston
Designed by Keith Groom
Printed in Hong Kong by the South China Printing Co.

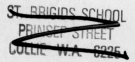

Previous page: A nesting mute swan surrounded by
her cygnets.

Animals

Most cities have a large well-stocked zoo. Lively monkeys, dignified lions and tigers, hugely impressive elephants and rhinos are among the most popular attractions. No wild place has such a wide variety of wild animals. Yet animals in the wild, although they are often difficult to find, are more interesting because they behave more naturally.

Animals are suited to the kind of places, or environments, they live in. A camel is well equipped to survive in the desert, a polar bear in the Arctic. The first part of this book introduces different environments and some of the animals that live in them.

We find some animals more attractive than others: furry koala bears, for example, are more endearing than venomous snakes. But life in the wild can be fierce and competitive. All animals have to eat to live. Some eat only plants. Others eat meat, and must prey on other animals. The last part of the book looks at how animals hunt their prey and defend themselves from attack.

An African elephant

Forest Animals

Ways of Life

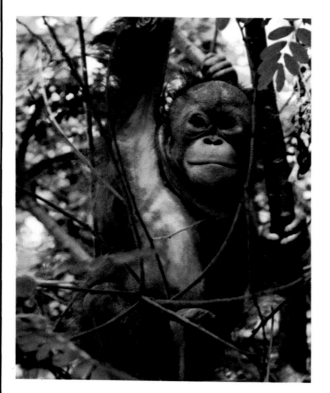

Woods and forests are full of life. Of course, the forests themselves *are* life — large trees, bushes, creepers and undergrowth plants. All this plant life provides plenty of food for animals.

The tropical rain forests of Africa, South America and Malaysia contain the greatest variety. Many thousands of animal species live in these great, steamy expanses of jungle. Rain-forest animals include the jaguar, which is a particular kind of large cat, as well as many kinds of colourful birds, apes and monkeys, and a multitude of snakes and insects.

Different sorts of animals live in the cooler forests away from the Tropics. Badgers, bears

◀ The orang-utan lives in the steamier rain forests of south-east Asia. It uses its long arms and gripping hands and feet to swing from tree to tree.

▼ Brown bears from the pine forests of Canada and Russia often catch their food from the forest streams and rivers.

and squirrels live in temperate forests, together with wood pigeons, woodpeckers and many other birds.

Although a forest may contain many animals, you could walk in one for an hour or more without noticing a single living creature, other than, perhaps, a bird or an insect. Forest animals are expert at concealing themselves among the leaves or undergrowth, either to escape from their enemies, or in readiness to pounce on an unsuspecting victim. For example, a chital deer is well concealed by its spotted coat among the undergrowth of its native Indian jungles, but its enemy the tiger is also well hidden by its stripes.

▼ These birds of paradise come from the jungles of New Guinea and Australia, where the dense foliage hides their brilliant colours.

◄ Most forest animals, such as this fruit-eating turaco from Africa, are the same colour as the trees they live in.

Desert Animals

◀ The Gila monster is a lizard that lives in desert country in the southern USA and northern Mexico. It is called a monster because it is one of the only two venomous lizards. The other is the beaded lizard which looks rather similar. These are slow-moving lizards, which use their poison to slow down and kill their speedier prey.

▶ For most snakes moving through the loose desert sand would be a problem. This desert viper manages because it has evolved a peculiar method of moving called sidewinding. Only two points on the under-side of the snake's body touch the sand at any one time. This gives the snake a better purchase or hold on the slippery sand. It also prevents the snake's body becoming over-heated from too much contact with the hot sand.

Deserts are generally very hot in the daytime but can be quite chilly at night. As this desert lizard warms up in the morning sun, it becomes more active.

When the sun gets too hot for the lizard's comfort, it seeks the cool of its burrow. There, it sleeps during the heat of the day, until the sun begins to set.

▶ The camel is well suited to desert life. Its feet splay out to bear its weight on the soft sand. Its long eyelashes keep fine sand out of its eyes. Its hump is a food store for long journeys.

If forests are crowded with animal life, then deserts, you might think, are empty of it. This is not so. Desert animals are not as numerous as forest animals but they are widespread and varied, and form thriving animal communities.

Most desert animals are small, although one or two such as the camel are large. All desert animals have evolved special ways of surviving in the hot, arid wastelands. Smaller desert animals often avoid the fierce heat of the daytime sun by burrowing underground or sheltering under stones. At night the desert comes to life as its animal inhabitants wake up and creep out from their holes and sheltering places.

Since plant life is so scarce, many animals are hunters, if only on a small scale. Desert foxes and snakes may like the taste of a fat gerbil or other desert rodent, but they may often have to be content with a few insects. The gerbil itself lives on stores of plant food – for even the desert blooms from time to time when it rains.

Then, the lizard comes out once more to feed. But the desert sands are still hot from the sun, so the lizard climbs on to a desert plant until the sand has cooled down.

The fennec is a little desert fox with very big ears. It uses them not only for listening out for its prey and for its enemies, but also for keeping cool in the hot desert climate. Big ears lose more heat than small ears. An Arctic fox has very small ears (see page 15), while a common red fox has medium-sized ears.

7

Plains Animals

Different countries have different sorts of plains, or large areas of flat land. In countries with cool or temperate climates and many rivers, the plains are usually green and fertile. In hotter countries with fewer rivers and lakes, plains are barer of grass and browner in colour. Sometimes they merge at their edges into dry, arid areas of scrub.

Populations of wild animals vary with the type of plains on which they live. The plains of northern Europe with their juicy grass

▼ Prairie dogs are not dogs but relatives of squirrels. They live in burrows on the North American plains.

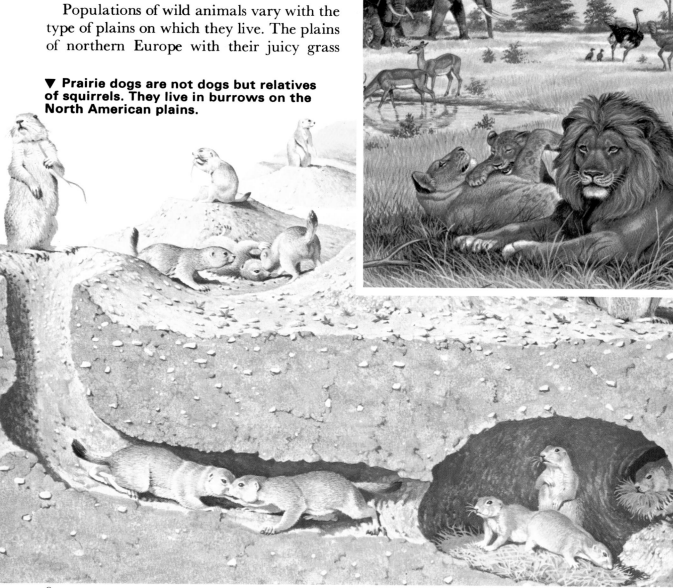

▼ This family of lions, and the elephants, antelope and ostriches in the background, live on the hot grassy plains, or savannah, of Africa.

are mainly grazed by domestic cattle and sheep, but wild animals such as rabbits and field mice live there too.

The grasslands of Africa look less lush, but are the home of many of the world's large animals. The coarse grass and small bushes provide food for large herds of zebras, antelopes and wildebeeste. Smaller groups of giraffes and elephants feed on the leaves of trees, while buffaloes and rhinos crop the grass. Lions are their largest enemies and await their chance to outrun and hunt down the weak or unwary.

The grasslands of several other countries are also hot and dry, but very different kinds of animals live on them, such as armadillos and giant anteaters in South America, and kangaroos, dingoes and rabbits in Australia.

▼ African rhinos are also savannah animals. This white rhino has a broad, flat mouth suitable for cropping grass close to the ground.

Mountain Animals

◀ An ibex eats almost any kind of plant food, and so can live high in the mountains even during winter, when the grass may be buried under snow.

▼ The mountain goat (left) and the chamois (right) are true mountain dwellers, confident and secure on the highest rock or narrowest ledge.

For an animal, mountain life has its advantages and its disadvantages. On the one hand, a true mountain animal, such as a chamois or other type of mountain goat, is safe from most enemies on its high crags. A smaller mountain animal, such as a marmot (very like the prairie dogs on the previous page) or a pika, can hide safely from attack among the many rocks and hollows of its mountain home.

On the other hand, high mountains are very harsh and inhospitable places, especially through their long, bitterly cold winters, when plant food is very scarce and

► Condors and eagles soar around mountain peaks looking with keen eyes for prey below. Here, a condor spreads its huge wings as it comes in to land on its high South American mountain home.

Pikas are close relatives of rabbits and hares. Many pikas live in cold, mountainous areas, where they feed by grazing the sparse cover of greenery, hiding behind the rocks from their enemies.

may be buried under thick snow. For this reason many mountain animals, including brown bears and mountain squirrels, hibernate or sleep through much of the winter, waking only at long intervals to forage for food.

An animal that lives on the steepest, rockiest parts of mountainsides has to be very sure-footed if it is not to fall and injure itself. A mountain goat is able to make dizzy leaps from crags to ledges and back again because its cloven hoofs have a very sure grip on the rockface. In winter the mountain goat is kept warm by its dense hairy coat. Also, like other kinds of goats, it is able to live off almost any kind of plant food.

Mountain birds have to contend with strong upcurrents and gales. Many small birds hop around in search of insects and seeds, but larger hawks and eagles are strong enough to use the upcurrents to soar among the mountain peaks. They have remarkable eyesight and swoop down to pick up rabbits, mice and smaller birds far below. Beetles, flies and mites can also survive mountain life, living on food such as pollen.

Ocean Animals

Seas and oceans cover more than two-thirds of the face of the Earth. In places the open ocean is deeper than most mountains are high. Peaks and valleys crinkle the ocean floor. Near the continents oceans are much shallower, and their floor is called the *continental shelf*.

Most marine plants and animals live in the upper sunlit layers of the sea. Here grow small drifting algae – green plants that furnish food for tiny drifting animals. Some of these tiny creatures are no bigger than a grain of rice. Some are the tiny young of barnacles, crabs, winkles, worms and starfish. Fish eggs and fry also form part of this animal life.

Together, the tiny plants and animals (called *plankton*) make the upper sea a nourishing 'soup' on which small fishes and other creatures feed. Mackerel and herring are among the many plankton eaters. But they, too, have their enemies. Mackerel and many other fishes are dark above and pale below. This makes it hard for predators to spot them. Also swimming in dense shoals helps such kinds of hunted fishes confuse their enemies. The flying fishes of warmer waters escape hunters by leaping from the sea and gliding perhaps 200 metres (660 ft) on wing-like fins.

However, hosts of creatures snap up fishes swimming in the upper levels of the sea. From above, gulls, albatrosses and other seabirds swoop to snatch up fishes such as herrings, pilchards, anchovies and sprats. Tuna and other bony fishes also prey on smaller creatures of their kind. Then, too, bony fishes are hunted by sharks and whales and the larger squids.

Deep down it is too dark for plants to grow. But there are fishes, such as deep-sea anglers and viper fish, and other animals that feed on the 'rain' of dead and dying creatures falling from above.

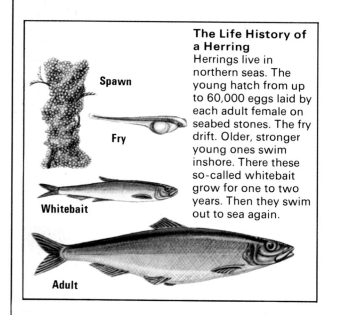

Spawn

Fry

Whitebait

Adult

The Life History of a Herring
Herrings live in northern seas. The young hatch from up to 60,000 eggs laid by each adult female on seabed stones. The fry drift. Older, stronger young ones swim inshore. There these so-called whitebait grow for one to two years. Then they swim out to sea again.

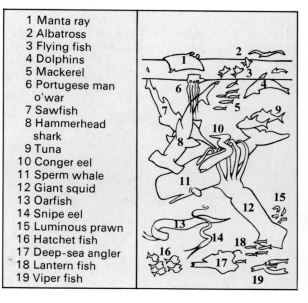

1 Manta ray
2 Albatross
3 Flying fish
4 Dolphins
5 Mackerel
6 Portugese man o'war
7 Sawfish
8 Hammerhead shark
9 Tuna
10 Conger eel
11 Sperm whale
12 Giant squid
13 Oarfish
14 Snipe eel
15 Luminous prawn
16 Hatchet fish
17 Deep-sea angler
18 Lantern fish
19 Viper fish

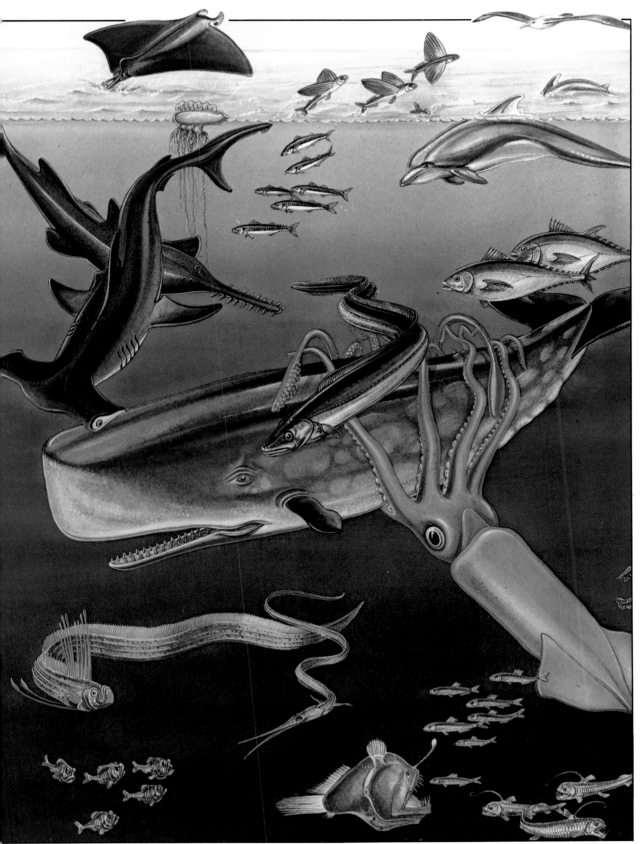

Life in the Cold

There is almost nowhere on the face of the Earth where animals do not live. Even deserts support animals which can withstand heat and drought.

The freezing wastelands of the Arctic regions are just as uninviting as the waterless deserts, but for different reasons. Here there is no shortage of fresh water. It is all around as snow and ice. But green plants, which provide so many animals with their food, are absent or rare in the white expanses of the Arctic and Antarctic continents. Only in the few weeks of summer do they grow at all, and then only around the fringes of these cold lands.

Life in polar regions depends on the sea. The freezing polar waters are very rich in plant life, the floating plankton. Plankton contains uncountable billions of tiny green plants and equally small animal life which feeds on these plants. In turn, these small animals are food for larger animals including the largest animals of all, the great baleen whales, which feed only on small shrimp-like krill.

Other large polar animals depend less directly on plankton. The polar bear kills seals for its food; the leopard seal skins and eats penguins. Other seals, and penguins, depend on fishes as their food. But all fishes depend, ultimately, on the plankton.

The Emperor penguin hatches its eggs by holding them off the snowy ground with its feet, keeping them warm against its body. When the eggs hatch, the penguin chicks are kept warm in the same way.

Small Life in the Arctic

Insects and other very small creatures depend largely on plant life, particularly flowers. When winter comes, most insects die off with the cold. So you might suppose that no insects live in the Arctic, a land of almost perpetual ice and snow. In fact, almost the opposite is true. During the short Arctic summer, when thick carpets of flowers spring up to cover very large areas, butterflies, flies, bees and other winged creatures can be seen feeding from the flowers. Arctic insects can produce such vast swarms that they become a plague both to Arctic animals and to the Eskimo and Lapp peoples. Great herds of caribou—first cousins of reindeer—roam the Canadian Arctic. In summer, the midges and mosquitoes pester them so much that they prefer to keep to the snow-covered areas where food is more scarce, rather than travel where food is plentiful but where the biting insects perpetually swarm.

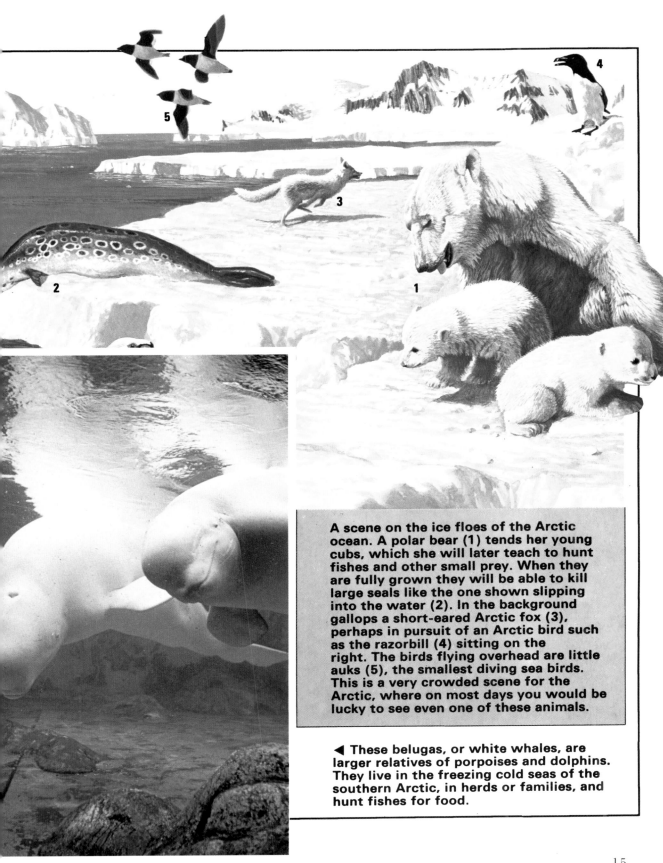

A scene on the ice floes of the Arctic ocean. A polar bear (1) tends her young cubs, which she will later teach to hunt fishes and other small prey. When they are fully grown they will be able to kill large seals like the one shown slipping into the water (2). In the background gallops a short-eared Arctic fox (3), perhaps in pursuit of an Arctic bird such as the razorbill (4) sitting on the right. The birds flying overhead are little auks (5), the smallest diving sea birds. This is a very crowded scene for the Arctic, where on most days you would be lucky to see even one of these animals.

◄ These belugas, or white whales, are larger relatives of porpoises and dolphins. They live in the freezing cold seas of the southern Arctic, in herds or families, and hunt fishes for food.

Fish Facts

The largest fish in the world is the whale shark, shown on the right. This great spotted monster grows up to 20 metres (66 feet) long and can weigh 70 tonnes—the weight of nine large elephants. Only the giant sea mammals, the great whales, are bigger than the whale shark. By contrast, the smallest of all fishes is probably the Luzon goby of the streams of South-East Asia. This is only just over a centimetre (less than 0·5 inches) long when fully grown.

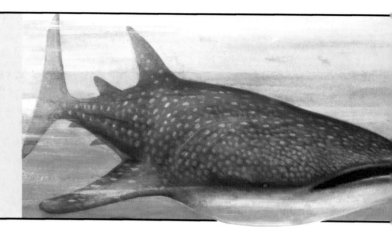

Record Rodents

The largest of all rodents or gnawing mammals is the capybara of South America. It is compared here with one of the smallest rodents, the harvest mouse.

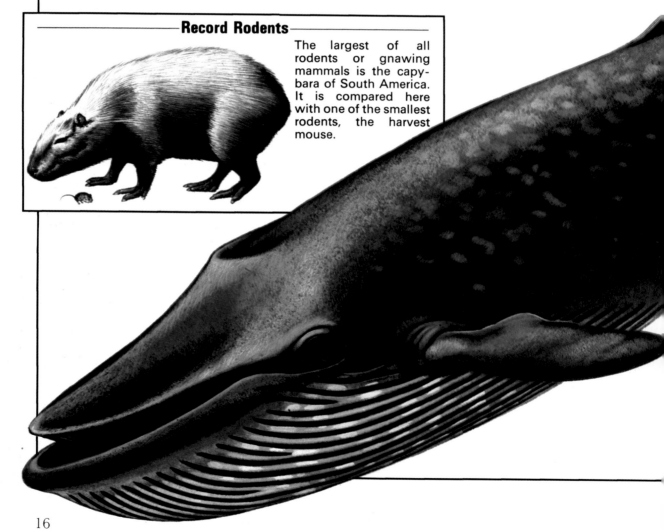

Animals

Biggest and Heaviest

Largest of All

The blue whale is the largest animal that has ever lived. It grows to over 30 metres (98 feet) long and weighs up to 140 tonnes—as much as 18 large elephants.

Giraffe
5½ metres high (18 feet)—tallest land animal.

Elephant
3·5 metres high (11·5 feet); weighs over 6 tonnes—heaviest land animal.

Reptile Records

● The biggest reptiles are salt-water crocodiles, which can be up to 6 metres (20 feet) long but are much thicker-bodied than snakes.
● Longest of all snakes is the anaconda of South America (right). It is the biggest of the boa family, thick-bodied snakes which crush their prey to death before swallowing it whole. Anacondas grow up to 10 metres (33 feet) or more long. The smallest snakes only grow up to 10 cm (4 inches) long.

Bird Facts

By far the largest of all living birds is the ostrich of the African plains. It stands nearly 2½ metres (8 feet) high and can weigh 140 kilogrammes (308 lb). Smaller, but still very large, flightless birds are the emu of Australia, the cassowary of New Guinea forests, and the rhea of South America. The smallest bird is the bee humming bird from Cuba. It is only 5 cm (2 inches) long and weighs about 2·8 grammes (0·1 ounces). The smallest European bird is the goldcrest at 14 grammes (0·5 ounces).

Fastest Movers

● Fastest land animal is the cheetah, which has been known to achieve a speed of 135 kph (84 mph)—faster than most motorists are allowed to go.

● Even speedier movers are some birds, notably the spine-tailed swift, which probably can dive at more than 300 kph (186 mph) and more usually flies at speeds over 140 kph (87 mph).

● The fastest snake is the black mamba, which is also one of the deadliest. However, as a fast mover perhaps it is a bit of a disappointment, because despite rumours of its being able to catch up with and attack a running man, it probably cannot travel at more than 11 kph (7 mph).

● The fastest creature in the oceans is the swordfish, which, surging through the surface layers in pursuit of its flying fish prey, can reach more than 90 kph (56 mph).

● But for their size, some insects are also very fast movers. A bee moves through the air at speeds up to 22 kph (14 mph), and a dragonfly can zip along at speeds up to 32 kph (20 mph). Insect wings beat at a tremendous rate—as many as 57,000 beats per minute.

Long Jumpers

Most famous of jumping animals are the kangaroos. A large kangaroo was once seen to make a jump of nearly 13 metres (43 feet). For its size, the tiny flea can make even more remarkable jumps, reaching as much as 25 cm (10 inches) in height, or 30 cm (12 inches) in length—about 200 to 300 times its own body length. Frogs, also famous jumpers, have been known to leap more than 5 metres (16 feet), or about 30 times their own length.

The white stork is a large bird that migrates from Europe to South Africa. It can only cross the sea at narrow channels.

The Arctic tern is the champion of all migratory birds, flying 16,000 kilometres (10,000 miles) between the polar regions.

The bobolink is a song bird which migrates between its breeding grounds in the north of Canada and the south of Argentina.

▶ The peregrine falcon is one of the fastest moving birds as it dives at 290 kph (180 mph), but the swift is even faster.

◀ The cheetah at full stretch is the fastest of all land animals.

Fastest and Farthest

Many animals need to be able to move very quickly. They include hunters chasing their prey, and prey escaping hunters. The cheetah, fastest of all land animals, is a hunter which attacks with a tremendous burst of speed, but gives up if it does not catch its prey within the first few minutes.

Other animals are capable of more sustained effort. Birds will often make migrations over vast distances, sometimes without seeming to take any rest. Hive insects such as ants, bees and wasps seem to be incessantly on the move, at least during the warm months of the year.

Long-distance Travellers

Many animals make migrations, or regular long-distance journeys from one place to another. They may be seeking the sun, as with the swallows that leave the shores of Europe in early autumn for the warmer ones of Africa. Or, like the caribou of Canada, they may make long journeys in search of food. Yet other animals migrate to faraway places to breed. The most famous example is the common eel, millions of which migrate every year across the Atlantic from their native European rivers to their spawning ground in the Sargasso Sea. Champion of all migrators, however, is the Arctic tern, a small bird that migrates the immense distance from the Arctic to the Antarctic and back every year.

Monarch butterflies migrate in enormous swarms from Canada to Mexico. Some of them drift out over the Pacific Ocean.

The common eel migrates thousands of kilometres from European rivers to spawn in the Sargasso Sea. The young eels then return to the same rivers.

Strange Animals

Many animals seem strange to us simply because we see them only very rarely, so they come as a great surprise to us when we do encounter them—usually at the zoo.

Some animals, though, really do live very strange lives. For example, the vampire bat shown in the photo lives entirely on blood, a way of life bizarre enough to have given rise to the Dracula legend.

Some animals are strange because they appear to be mixtures of other animals. The most famous example is the platypus shown below. This is really a primitive sort of warm-blooded mammal but it has many of the features of a cold-blooded reptile.

Even animals which are more or less familiar to us may have odd features to their lives. Most people know what a kangaroo looks like, but very few have seen a newborn kangaroo, which is very tiny, blind and hairless. Despite its apparent helplessness —it is only about a centimetre (half an inch) long—a newborn kangaroo finds it own way to its mother's pouch.

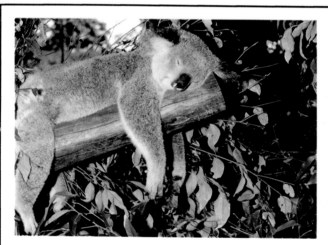

Australian Oddities

◄ Koalas eat only eucalyptus leaves. This koala snoozes peacefully in its home tree. It spends the first six months of its life in its mother's pouch, the next six clinging to her back.

► A young kangaroo, or joey, sucks milk from the teat inside its mother's pouch.

◄ The platypus is a very strange animal. It has a flat tail and webbed feet like a beaver, but a horny bill like a duck. It has hair like a mammal, yet it lays eggs like a reptile. Also like a mammal, it feeds its young on milk—but the milk oozes out of slits, not teats as in other mammals.

▼ The pangolin, shown stretched out on a branch and also curled up asleep, is another eater of ants and termites. Unlike all other mammals, its body is covered by large scales, so that it looks rather like a long, active pine cone!

▲ Most bats eat insects, but this vampire bat drinks only blood. In its tropical American home, a vampire sucks blood from larger animals and people, but this captive bat sips its blood from a bottle-top. This strange-looking creature was the inspiration for the fictional character Count Dracula, who lived on human blood and turned his victims into vampires too.

The axolotl normally never grows into an adult. It is a giant tadpole which lives in water all its life, breathing through gills. In captivity, however, it can be made to lose its gills and turn into a land-living salamander.

▶ The aardvark is a South African animal that lives on termites. It digs these little creatures out from their hard-walled nests with its tremendously strong claws, and licks them up in thousands with its long thin tongue.

▲ The North American buffalo or bison was hunted almost to extinction in the last century.

▲ American alligators were once hunted for their hide. Now, they are being killed off by water pollution.

▼ The sea otter was almost wiped out for its beautiful fur. It is now protected.

▲ The Californian condor, largest American bird of prey, has been hunted nearly to extinction.

▲ The rock fowl lives in West African forests. But these are rapidly being felled.

▼ The Caspian tiger was once common in the northern forests of Iran but may now be completely extinct in the wild.

▲ The Spanish lynx is fast disappearing because of gun-toting hunters and poisoned bait left by farmers.

▲ The Spanish eagle is another noble bird of prey threatened by farmers and hunters.

◄ The Komodo dragon is the world's largest living lizard—but it is under threat.

▼ The thylacine, or marsupial wolf, of Australia, has been hunted almost to extinction.

Animals under Threat

In the last century the great plains of North America swarmed with hundreds of millions of buffalo. Gross over-hunting has now reduced these great animals to a few carefully preserved herds.

A hundred years ago, only a few explorers had penetrated the vast expanses of the Brazilian rain forests. But this great jungle of unique animals and plants has now been invaded by human beings and their destructive machines, so that forest animals and plants are fast disappearing.

Of course, many kinds of animals and plants (in fact, *millions* of kinds) became extinct, or disappeared from the face of the Earth, long before human beings ever inhabited it. The dinosaurs, for example, ruled the Earth in vast numbers and variety for more than 150 million years, but despite their great and lasting success, they disappeared completely.

Today, it is the turn of the animals who succeeded the dinosaurs—the mammals, the birds, and the few remaining large reptiles—to come under threat of extinction. This threat comes mostly from people, who are now by far the most common large animal. As they change the Earth to suit themselves, they make it harder and harder for any other large animal, except domestic animals, to survive. We now realize that all wild animals are a valuable part of life, and try to conserve them. Many kinds of threatened animals are protected by law from being hunted and killed. Special wildlife reserves have also been set up.

Elephants in London Zoo.

Zoos

We see most wild animals in the zoo. When zoos first became popular, about a century ago, many kinds of animals could not be persuaded to breed and died after only a short while in captivity. With experience, zookeepers learned much more about the particular needs of wild animals. Today, animals in zoos live much longer and more of them are able to raise their young there. Some wild animals, though, still cannot survive easily in a zoo, which is why you will not usually find koala bears or platypuses there. Such delicate animals are often protected inside special nature reserves. Herds of much larger animals such as elephants and rhinos, are conserved inside game-parks or safari parks.

Predators

Tooth and Claw

▼ Although it is smaller than a lion or a tiger, the leopard is a mighty hunter. In fact, for its size it is the most powerful of all the great cats. Only a leopard has the strength to spring up into a tree holding prey as heavy as itself.

Hidden by leaves on a branch, a leopard waits to leap down on to the back of an unsuspecting forest gazelle. In the dusk an owl flits noiselessly over the meadows, its great eyes keeping a sharp lookout for signs of a mouse moving in the grass.

These are examples of solitary hunting animals, or predators, seeking their prey. But no animal can live entirely alone. Even lone predators are usually hunting for the whole family. They return with their catches to a nest or hideout where their hungry young are waiting.

Each kind of animal has its own way of defending itself from attack. Some are armed with sharp horns or lethal stings. Others can run so fast they cannot be caught. They may also rely on safety in numbers, and keep together in herds.

▲ Antelopes usually keep together in herds. A hunting animal will not attack a large group, but this antelope may have strayed too far away from the rest of the herd. Or it may have been too weak or sick to keep up as the herd ran from the prowling leopard.

and Prey

▼ Small but fierce—a Little Owl returns to its nest in an English wood with a large moth in its beak.

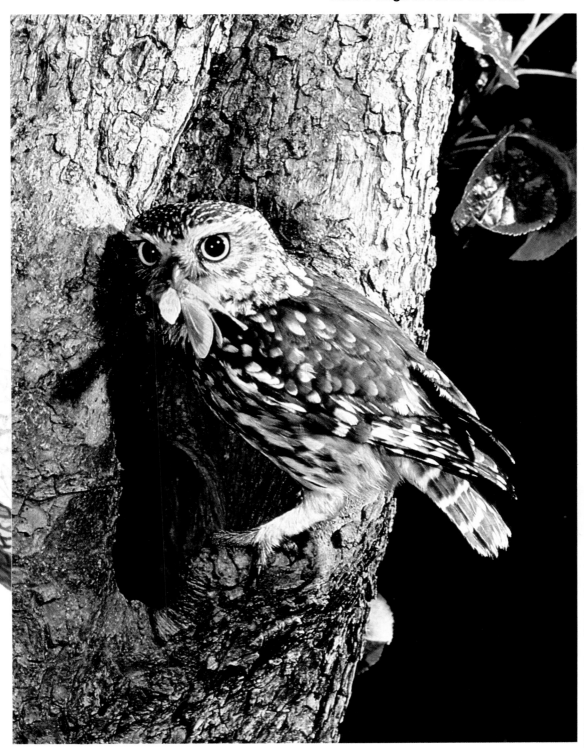

Hunters

Large predators may have to hunt over a very wide area to catch their prey. An eagle may soar over thousands of square kilometres in a week's hunting. A tiger will often scour a hundred kilometres of jungle pathways in search of a single meal.

Other big predators, however, may stay more or less in the same place, day after day, simply waiting for their prey to turn up. This is true of alligators and crocodiles, who often drag their prey into the water of their native rivers to drown it before eating it. Giant snakes such as boas and anacondas lurk in wait for long periods for their prey. They are predators without being really active hunters.

Some predators, however, usually hunt in groups or families. Wolves and wild dogs hunt in packs. In lion families, lionesses normally do the hunting together. After the kill has been made the male lions often collect the first share and the best pickings.

In the oceans, killer whales are the most ferocious predators that hunt in family packs. They often attack great, harmless whales many times their own considerable size, tearing out the whales' huge tongues as the tastiest part of their bodies, before killing them. Yet these same killer whales, in captivity, are quite gentle with their human trainers.

▼ **The golden eagle nests on high mountain ledges throughout the Northern Hemisphere. It is the largest bird of prey in the British Isles. It seizes its prey, such as hares and ptarmigan, in its long sharp talons.**

Most predators rely on such weapons as sharp teeth and claws, but some employ venom or poison as their main weapon. Most well known, of course, are the venomous snakes, who have special teeth which inject the venom into their prey. The snake is then able to eat the paralysed or dead prey at leisure. Two kinds of lizards, the Gila monster and the beaded lizard, are also venomous. Many insect predators have poison jaws or stings with which they paralyse or kill their prey.

▼ A venomous bird-eating spider from the tropical jungles.

Not all predators are large animals, of course. A weasel is a very small but extremely ferocious predator, which can kill a rabbit up to twenty times as heavy as itself, with a bite on the back of the neck. Spiders are perhaps the most familiar small predators, whether waiting in the centre of a web for the arrival of insect prey, as in the case of the garden spider, or out actively hunting it, like the wolf spiders. The bird-eating spider of the tropical rain forests is much larger—about the same size as the small birds on which it preys. Piranha fishes are small, sharp-toothed predators which hunt in shoals and can soon strip a large animal to the bone.

Most feared of all hunters of the sea are the great killer sharks. Fast swimmers that hunt by scent, they can inflict terrible injuries on unwary seaside bathers, sometimes biting off whole limbs. Although many sharks may attack at once, they are not really pack animals. A shark is a solitary hunter that will attack anything that smells of blood—including any other wounded shark.

Defence and Disguise

Predatory animals do not have things all their own way. Their prey are not weak and defenceless. Most are well equipped to escape their attacker's hungry jaws, and healthy antelopes are fast enough to escape a hunting lion. A grown African buffalo is more than a match for any lion, and few predators will attack a porcupine.

These wild animals rely on speed, strength and armour (horns), and weapons (long, barbed quills) to defend themselves. But many other animals use defences that are much less obvious—that are, in fact, disguises.

The best-known kind of disguise is camouflage. This is any type of colouring and patterning which makes the animal less visible against its background. The zebra's

▲ The porcupine fish normally has an average fish-shape, but when it is frightened or menaced it puffs itself up like this to become more difficult to swallow.

Some insect disguises: The green bush cricket (1) is camouflaged by colour. The leaf insect (2), the stick insect (3), the thorn-tree hopper (4) and the leaf butterfly (5), as their names suggest, match their surroundings perfectly. By contrast the wasp (6), the cinnabar moth (7) and the puss moth caterpillar (8) use bright colours to warn predators to keep away.

The brilliant colours of this little South American tree frog warn of its extreme poisonousness. Its only enemies are forest Indians, who capture and kill it for its deadly poison, which they will then use to tip their arrows. One scratch from such an arrow will bring a monkey toppling down from a tree.

▲ With its armoury of long, sharp, barbed quills, a porcupine is safe from attack—even from lions, unless they are very hungry indeed.

▲ Predators as well as prey use camouflage to remain unseen. Although this tiger is visible enough in the open, its stripes will conceal it in longer grass.

stripes and the giraffe's brown and white pattern make them harder to see in the African trees and grasses. Many insects, such as greenfly, grasshoppers and crickets, are green, and so are hard to see among green leaves and grass. Other insects are shaped as well as coloured to resemble the plant on which they live. If the leaf insect, stick insect, thorn-tree hopper and leaf butterfly were not numbered in the diagram, they would be very difficult to spot.

Instead of disguising themselves, some prey animals, such as the wasp and cinnabar moth, look as visible as possible by means of bright, staring colours, usually yellow, black and red. These colours warn a predator that the animal stings or tastes nasty, and the predator learns to leave it alone. The puss moth can in addition squirt a pungent liquid at any enemy rash enough to attack it.

Even 'cleverer' prey animals come to resemble these nasty-tasting species, so that predators leave them alone too, even though they don't taste nasty or sting. A hoverfly, for example, looks very like a wasp.

Scavengers

Nothing is wasted in the wild. After a large predator, such as a lion or tiger, has made its kill and eaten its fill, perhaps only some skin and bone remains of its prey. But even this will soon disappear after the scavengers have got to work.

These are the tidiers-up of nature. Not only do they remove bits of animals that have been killed as prey, but they also eat and dispose of the bodies of creatures who have died of disease, or old age, or as the result of a fall or other accident. Some scavengers specialize in removing and eating the dung that larger animals drop.

Scavenging may seem an unpleasant way of life. Obviously the scavengers themselves do not think so—a bit of really smelly carrion appeals to a scavenger as a really tasty meal. And scavenging is vital. Just think of what would happen if all the skin and bones, all the dead bodies, and all the dung in nature just lay around and piled up!

At one time, it was thought that the hyena, a large meat-eater, lived entirely by scavenging. Its jaws are powerful enough to crack the thickest and strongest bones left behind by the lion. But now we know that the hyena often makes its own kills—which the lion is not averse to scavenging.

Not all scavengers are large. Jackals, foxes and vultures are medium-sized animals. Others are small. These include many little fishes (the oceans need tidying up too) and the scarab, or dung, beetles pictured on page 31.

But the most important scavengers of all are much too small to be seen without a microscope. These are the bacteria and fungi that cause decay, and so return all once-living things back to the soil to provide plants with their vital mineral food.

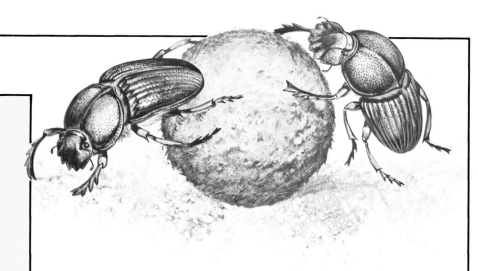

◄ The spotted hyena is a large scavenger which eats carrion and even dung. But it also preys on zebras and antelopes.

▶ These scarab beetles are scavenging dung, which they form into a ball to roll away to their nest as food for their grubs.

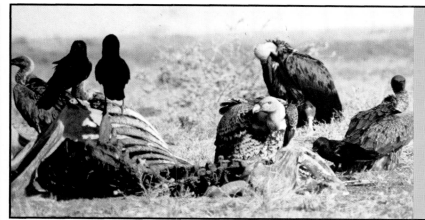

◄ On this large carcass lying on the hot African grasslands are perched two types of medium-sized scavengers—vultures and ravens. What little they leave will be finished off by beetles and other very small scavengers.

▼ The marabou is a rather ugly stork that specializes in scavenging.

◄ The fox once hunted only in the countryside but has now become a town scavenger. Being an intelligent animal, it knows what good pickings are to be had from overfull dustbins!

The Nile crocodile is the greatest and most ferocious of living reptiles, yet it allows these small birds to roam about its body and even inside its fearsomely toothed jaws. The reason is that the birds eat parasites and dead skin, so helping both themselves and the crocodile. This is a form of symbiosis.

Together

This cuckoo, being fed by its host or foster parent, a dunnock, is a parasite. As an egg it was laid in the foster parents' nest. Now it is the only chick remaining alive, and is much bigger than the host birds that have to feed it. This is very unusual among parasites, which are nearly all much smaller than their hosts.

Baboon Family Life

Baboons are monkeys that live mostly on the ground, in large families or troops. They lead a very definite family life in which everyone has his or her special position and duties. These are shown in the picture by colours. The large adult male baboons, shown pale blue, are the guardians and fathers of the troop. They defend the troop against enemies. One adult male usually acts as lookout when the troop is feeding, and barks a warning if a fast escape is necessary. Each adult male has several mates, shown light brown. These may have one, or unusually two, small baby baboons clinging to them, shown red. Older juveniles, dark blue, often leave their mothers to play in groups. Adolescents, shown dark brown, help forage for food and keep a lookout.

Grooming is important in keeping the troop together. One of these females is grooming her husband, but all ranks except the small babies will groom other troop members. Grooming is both comforting and cleaning.

Symbiosis

Symbiosis is the closest kind of living together. Neither partner in the symbiosis can live easily, or at all, without the other. To take the example of the crocodile and the cleaner-birds shown on the left: without the crocodile the birds could not get their food, and without the cleaner-birds the crocodile's skin would soon become infested with parasites.

Other symbiotic partnerships may be even closer. Small insects called termites live in large colonies and often eat wood. But they are unable to digest this without microscopic, one-celled protozoa which live inside their bodies. Neither termite nor protozoa can live without the other. But protozoa which live inside animals can also cause disease—for example, malaria. Many helpful symbionts have turned into harmful parasites, and *vice versa*.

Some animals are hunters while others are hunted. But mainly, wild animals live together in nature. Even predators and their prey, such as the lions, zebras and antelopes on the African plains, live peaceably together for most of the time. Except at hunting time, they take little notice of one another.

Some animals live very close together, in families. Such are the lions and the monkey families, including the baboon troop described on these pages. Family life is more complicated than herd life, and family animals are generally more intelligent than herd animals.

Different kinds of animals may depend upon one another for a living or a useful service. One example of this is the crocodile and cleaner-birds shown in the picture. Or, one animal may be a harmful parasite of another, as the cuckoo is of the dunnock and many other small birds.

Animal Homes

Many creatures lack permanent homes. Most fishes just sleep where they happen to be. But some animals make or use homes where they sleep, hide from predators, or raise families.

The home may be a ready-made shelter. Thus the moray eel hides in a gap between the rocks on the seabed. A lion may sleep by a boulder. Bats roost in the dark safety of caves.

Other homes are holes dug in soil, wood or rock. Rabbits and prairie dogs (see page 8) burrow into the ground. The grubs of furniture beetles live snugly in tunnels bored through timber. Some worms of sandy shores dwell in underground caves lined with sticky mucus to stop the walls falling in.

Yet other animals build shelters above ground. The gorilla sleeps on a rough, leafy platform. Beavers construct big mud-and-stick homes. Certain insects, fishes and birds build homes with astonishing care. Yet their skills are not learnt – they work entirely by instinct.

Animals tend to fight creatures of their own kind if these come too near to their homes. Even animals without homes will defend their own territory – the patch of land or water they live in. A lizard's territory may be no more than a bush. A puma might claim a region more than 40 kilometres (25 miles) across. Marking the edge of its territory with scent is one way in which a creature may warn off rivals. Foxes and dogs behave in this way.

Homes and defended territories help to make safe places where animals can raise their young. Some take far greater care of their offspring than others. Most sea fishes hatch from myriads of eggs shed haphazardly into the water. But many fishes that lay fewer eggs show more concern. Male sticklebacks build nests where the females lay eggs. The males guard the young until they swim freely.

▲ No insect home builder is more ingenious than the weaver ant, which lives in trees. Hundreds pull leaves toward each other. Then worker ants grasp ant grubs in their jaws and move them to and fro between the leaves. A silk thread comes from each grub's mouth. With this the workers weave the leaf edges together to make a 'Chinese lantern' nest.

▲ In summer, the dormouse gathers moss and leaves and builds a snug nest for its young. The nest has a side entrance and is usually well hidden in bushes.

◀ Potter wasps mould mud and sand into hollow 'pots' which hang from plants like strange fruit. The female lays her eggs in these pots, one in each. She then attacks a caterpillar, which she paralyzes with her sting. The female stuffs the still living victim in her nest as fresh food for her grubs when they hatch.

Ants and many bees have workers to tend their nurseries.

Most reptiles and amphibians give no aid to their own eggs or young. They may even eat them. But birds hatch eggs with the warmth from their bodies, and bring food to the hatchlings. Mammals suckle their young. Some apes feed and protect their offspring for years, and teach them to look after themselves.

◀ The ovenbird of South America uses mud, grass and leaves to build a nest rather like an old-fashioned oven. It lays its eggs inside on a soft bed of grass.

▶ A baby kangaroo has a mobile home. It has free rides and a warm home in its mother's pouch until it is quite large.

▼ Beavers are the master builders of the animal world. They are widespread in North America, and a few still live in Eurasia. Several beavers build a dam across a stream, creating a large pond. This keeps them safe from predators. Behind the dam they build homes, called 'lodges' out of sticks and mud. A lodge has a number of entrance tunnels underwater, and a single room above the water level for living. Each lodge is home for a single family.

Escaping Winter

When frost grips the land in winter many animals face problems. Cold-blooded creatures lose the energy needed to stay active. Warm-blooded animals may run short of food. Animals overcome these difficulties in various ways.

Some animals hibernate – or sleep away the winter. Dormice, hedgehogs and bats are among many hibernators. In autumn most seek out some frost-free shelter. There, their body temperature falls, their heart beat slows down and a long gap separates each breath from the next. Frogs and terrapins that spend the winter under water stop breathing altogether. Their skins absorb what little oxygen they need from the oxygen dissolved in water. Certain butterflies and snakes also go to sleep for the winter.

A hibernating animal can live for months without a meal. This is partly because it uses up so little energy, and partly because it lives off body fat stored up in summer.

Not all creatures need to hibernate to get away from winter. The little Arctic rodents known as lemmings live in runways under the snow, feeding on plants that grow there.

Other Arctic mammals wander south when winter closes in. Among these are Europe's reindeer and North America's caribou. Herds trudge up to 1300 kilometres (800 miles) every autumn to reach their winter feeding grounds.

But such journeys are short trips compared with the migrations of some insects, fishes and birds.

Some butterflies flutter all the way from Canada and the United States to Mexico to spend the winter.

Birds are the champion long-distance travellers. Each autumn millions wing their way thousands of miles from northern breeding grounds to warmer winter quarters. The following spring, the birds return. See also pages 18 and 19.

Bats

Snake

You do not see many animals during the winter because they have hidden away somewhere and are asleep. This winter sleep is called hibernation. Here animals hibernate in their winter homes, waiting for the warmer days of spring. But some animals that sleep a lot in winter do not truly hibernate. The bear and squirrel, for instance, come out on mild days to find food. Cold-blooded creatures, like snakes, tortoises and frogs only hibernate in cold countries. In hot countries, there is no need for them to hibernate.

Squirrel

Brown bear

Hedgehog

Frog

Tortoise

Dormouse

Earthworm

Animals and Plants

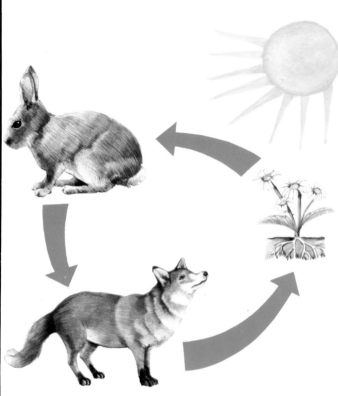

All animal life depends, finally, on plant life. This fox feeds on the rabbit and the rabbit feeds on the green plant. But the green plant, to build up its own body, needs only mineral salts and water from the soil, carbon dioxide from the air, and energy from the Sun.

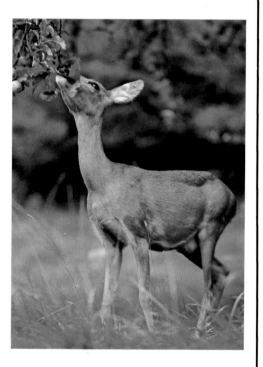

▶ A red-deer doe nibbles at tree leaves. This kind of plant-eating is called browsing, whereas nibbling grass and other ground plants is called grazing.

You usually find most animals where there are most plants. For example, a patch of grassland or jungle contains more wild animals than the same area of desert or high mountain.

As shown in the diagram above, green plants are what make animal life possible. This is so even in the oceans, where very few green plants, except a few floating seaweeds, are to be seen. The vast majority of oceanic plants are very tiny, often consisting of only a single living cell. These are the green plants of the plankton, the almost invisible floating life of the oceans. Larger oceanic animals feed on the tiny plankton, plants and animals. Still larger animals eat *them*, and so on. This is called a food chain.

Food chains also occur in life on land. The diagram shows a simple food chain: plant-rabbit-fox. A rather longer food chain is plant-beetle-bird-wild cat. There are many others.

Index

Acknowledgements

Photographs: 4 NHPA/Philip Wayre; 6 NHPA/K. H. Switak; 9 SATOUR; 10 Zefa; 15 Pat Morris; 17 NHPA; 20 C. R. Roberts *top,* Zefa *bottom;* 21 Pat Morris *top* and *centre;* 24 Zoological Society of London/Michael Lyster; 25 NHPA; 26 NHPA; 27 Seaphot; 28 Seaphot/Christian Petron; 29 Zoological Society of London *top,* NHPA *bottom;* 30 Pat Morris, 30/1 NHPA; 31 Pat Morris *centre,* NHPA *bottom;* 33 NHPA; 38 Zefa.

Picture research: Penny Warn.